Girls Just Like You

BIBLE WOMEN WHO TRUSTED GOD

Copyright © Jean Stapleton 2017
ISBN: 978-1-78191-997-2
10 9 8 7 6 5 4 3 2 1
Published by Christian Focus Publications Ltd,
Geanies House, Fearn, Tain, Ross-shire,
IV20 1TW, Scotland, U.K.
Tel: 01862 871011
Fax: 01862 871699
www.christianfocus.com
email: info@christianfocus.com

Cover design by Tom Barnard
Cover and inside illustrations by Jeff Anderson
Printed and bound in China

Girls Just Like You

Like You

BIBLE WOMEN WHO TRUSTED GOD

Jean Stapleton

CF4·K

CONTENTS

Just Like You

'Elijah was a man with a nature like ours ...' James 5:17

In the Bible we read about men and women who God chose for some special work. Elijah was a prophet: God spoke to Elijah so that he could tell the people what God wanted them to know. God also helped Elijah to do wonderful things, so that the people would know that the words he spoke really were from God.

We might think that people like Elijah were different from us, much braver than we are. But our verse today teaches us that Elijah was like us. He could feel afraid or tired or lonely like we do. Elijah trusted God and obeyed God. He believed that God would give him strength to do the things He asked him to do.

In this book we will learn about some of the women in the Bible, who trusted God like Elijah did. There is much more to read in the Bible about these women. I hope that you will soon be able to read more for yourself.

THINK AND PRAY: Praying to God is important. Pray that God will help you to learn something each day about what it means to trust Him.

DAY 1

Sarai Leaves Her Home

Read: Genesis 12:1

Sarai lived about two thousand years before Jesus was born in Bethlehem. She was married to Abram and their home was in the city of Ur. This city was in the country now called Iraq.

One day Sarai knew that she must leave her home in Ur. She did not know where she was going to live. God had spoken to Abram and had told him he must leave the place where he was living. God promised that many people would come from Abram's family. He also promised that families all over the world would be blessed (made happy) by Abram's family.

Abram and Sarai obeyed God. They set out, not knowing where God wanted them to go. Abram's father, Terah, and Abram's brother's son, Lot, went with them. They travelled many miles up a river valley to the city of Haran. The journey would have taken a long time, with no cars or trains or aeroplanes. They may have used camels to carry them and their belongings. They stayed in Haran until Abram's father died.

Sarai had to get ready to travel again. She was about sixty-five years old and Abram was ten years older than her. But they needed to find the place where God wanted them to live. They took another long journey, this time into the land of Canaan.

God spoke to Abram again. God told Abram that He would give the land of Canaan to his family. Sarai no longer had a house to live in. She would have to get used to living in a tent. Abram became rich, with many animals, and with silver and gold. But Abram and Sarai never lived in a house in Canaan.

THINK AND PRAY: Sarai travelled many miles to a land she was not used to. She and her husband did this because they obeyed God. Ask God to help you obey Him.

DAY 2

Sarah's Baby Boy

Read: Genesis 21:6

Sarah did not find it easy to believe God's promise that this family would grow into many people. She was getting older and she had no children. Many years went by, and God promised that Sarah would have a son. It was hard for her to believe this. She was so much older than a mother usually is when her baby is born. But God had even told Abraham what their baby's name should be: Isaac. (The name Isaac means 'laughter'.)

When Sarah was ninety years old, her baby was born. Abraham and Sarah called him Isaac as God had said they should. Sarah's life had not been easy. She had travelled from her home in the city. She had lived for twenty-five years in a tent, learning the ways of a different land. She had waited so long for this promised baby. What a happy time for her now, with her little boy to care for.

Sarah had a long time of learning to trust God. She learned that God always does what He promises. She also must have learned that there was something very special about Isaac's birth. The promises that God had given to Abraham, about this family, would belong to Isaac too.

Do you remember God's promise about Abraham's family doing good to families all over the world? In your Bible, find Matthew chapter 1 verses 1-2, and verse 16. God's promise to Abraham and then to Isaac, was all about the Lord Jesus. He is the Son of God. He is the only person born into the world who never sinned (did anything that is wrong).

When the Lord Jesus died on the cross, He took the punishment for the sin of everyone who trusts in Him. This is the good news for families everywhere.

THINK AND PRAY: We are all sinners. Jesus is the only person without sin. When you pray today, ask God to help you to understand why the Lord Jesus came.

DAY 3

Rebekah at the Well

Read: Genesis 24:1-4

Rebekah lived in Haran with her parents and her brother Laban. Her life was very different from ours today. She could not turn on the tap when she needed water to drink or for cooking or washing. Water had to be carried from a well, where it was brought up from deep in the ground. She would have been used to seeing travellers arrive on camels.

One day, when Rebekah went to the well, she saw some strangers. One man politely asked her for a drink. Rebekah gave him some water and then brought enough water from the well for all his ten camels. The man gave her a present and asked her about her family. Who could this man be?

The man by the well was Abraham's servant. The verses you read today, were about Abraham sending his most trusted servant on the long journey to Haran. This was to find the right wife for Isaac. Abraham and Sarah did not want Isaac to marry a woman from Canaan who worshipped idols. (An idol is like a statue made of gold or silver, wood or stone. It can be like a person, an animal or even like the sun or the moon.) Abraham sent his servant to Haran because that was where his relations lived.

Rebekah did not know that while the servant waited at the well, he had prayed. He had asked God to help him to find the right wife for Isaac. He prayed that when he asked for a drink, if the woman brought enough water for all the camels as well, she would be the one.

The man had hardly finished praying, when Rebekah came and did exactly that. When the servant asked Rebekah about her family, she told him that Abraham's brother Nahor, was her grandfather.

The servant thanked God for leading him to Abraham's relations.

THINK AND PRAY: God has given us lots of good things, hasn't he? Think of them, then remember to thank God for His goodness, like Abraham's servant did.

DAY 4

Rebekah's Journey

Read: Genesis 24:42-46

Rebekah's brother, Laban, invited Abraham's servant and the men who were with him, to come into the house. The camels were given food and made comfortable, and a meal was prepared for the men.

Abraham's servant would not eat until he had told the family why he had come. He told them about Abraham and Sarah and Isaac. He explained that it was important to Abraham that Isaac married the right woman.

The verses you read today tell us how the servant had prayed as he waited by the well. When they heard about this, Rebekah's father Bethuel and her brother Laban were sure that God had chosen Rebekah to be Isaac's wife. Once again the servant gave thanks to God. He then gave presents to Rebekah and to her brother and her mother.

The next morning, after a night's rest, Abraham's servant wanted to start the journey back. Rebekah's mother and her brother wanted Rebekah to stay with her family for a few more days. When they saw how much the servant wanted to return to Abraham, they decided to ask Rebekah. Rebekah said that she would go.

In those days, people had servants to work for them and help them. So Rebekah's maids and her nurse (who would have looked after her when she was small) went with her. They had a long journey ahead as they set off on the camels.

Rebekah had never met Isaac. She and her family believed that God had chosen her to be Isaac's wife. She was willing to trust God.

THINK AND PRAY: When you are worried and anxious do you bring your troubles to God? You may never have such an exciting journey as Rebekah's, but pray that you may always trust God to take care of you.

DAY 5

Shiphrah and Puah

Read: Exodus 1:15-16

When a baby is born, there is a special nurse who takes care of the baby, and the mother. The nurse who does this is called a midwife.

A long time ago, in the land of Egypt, there were two midwives whose names were Shiphrah and Puah. They were not Egyptians, they were Israelites. The Israelites came from the family of Jacob (Abraham's grandson). Jacob's son Joseph had saved the Egyptians from starving, when there was a famine in the land. Jacob and all his family came to live in Egypt. At that time there were seventy people in Jacob's family.

Jacob's twelve sons all had children of their own. Those children grew up and got married and more children were born.

A new Pharaoh (the King) who had not known Joseph, looked at the part of the land that had been given to Jacob's family. He saw lots of Israelites living there.

He didn't like to see so many people in Egypt who were not Egyptians. He thought that one day the Israelites might fight against the Egyptians.

Pharaoh decided to give the Israelites lots of hard work to do. They were made to build cities for the Egyptians. But still lots of Israelite children were born.

Pharaoh sent for Shiphrah and Puah. He told them that when one of the Israelite mothers had a baby girl, the baby could live. But when a baby boy was born, they must not let him live.

What could the midwives do? They did not want to harm any little babies. If they disobeyed Pharaoh, they could be punished.

THINK AND PRAY: Do your friends ever ask you to do something you know you shouldn't? If you are ever asked to do something that is wrong, pray that God will help you to do right.

DAY 6

Learning from Shiphrah and Puah

Read: Exodus 1:17

When a baby is born, the midwife will make sure it is healthy. She will make sure the baby is breathing properly and is nice and warm. She will also help the mother to care for her baby.

Shiphrah and Puah knew what should be done to help a new baby, whether it was a boy or a girl, and how to help the mother. They didn't want to do anything that could harm the new baby. They also knew that it is God who gives life. God had said that no one should take away another person's life (Genesis chapter 9). We all know that this is right.

Shiphrah and Puah had to choose whether to obey God or to obey Pharaoh. They knew that they must obey God, even if Pharaoh was angry with them.

Pharaoh sent for them. He knew that they were saving the little boys, as well as the little girls. Shiphrah and

Puah explained that the Israelite babies were born so quickly that they did not get there in time. The babies were born while they were on their way to help.

THINK AND PRAY: Pharaoh was very powerful and could have put Shiphrah and Puah in prison or even put them to death. But these two women trusted God and did what was right. There are people we should obey: our parents, our schoolteachers, and people who are in charge of the country we live in. It sometimes happens that someone we usually obey, tells us to do something we know is wrong. The true story of Shiphrah and Puah teaches us that if we are told to do something that God says is wrong, we must obey God. Pray that God will show you what is right and wrong and that you will have the strength to obey His Word.

DAY 7

Jochebed's Baby Boy

Read: Exodus 2:1-3

Jochebed and her husband Amram were Israelites who lived in the land of Egypt. They had two children: a boy called Aaron and his sister Miriam. Then a new baby was expected. As the family waited they must have wondered, as all families do, would this baby be a boy or a girl?

When a baby is born, it is usually a very happy time for the family. But for the Israelites it was a frightening time. Pharaoh knew that the Israelite midwives saved the baby boys as well as the baby girls. He told all the Egyptians that when an Israelite boy was born, he must be killed. You will remember that Pharaoh was afraid of having too many Israelites in his land.

Jochebed's baby was a boy. He was beautiful. Jochebed kept him hidden until he was three months old. It is very difficult to keep a baby hidden. What if he cried

and someone heard him? Jochebed knew that she could not hide her baby any longer.

Bulrushes grew beside the river. One day Jochebed gathered some bulrushes. At home, she wove them into a basket. She covered the basket with something that would keep water out. Then she put the baby into the basket. Jochebed went down to the river. She carried the basket with her. and placed it among the reeds near the bank of the river. Miriam kept watch to see what would happen to her baby brother.

Jochebed had done everything she could to keep her baby safe. God was helping her to do what was best, as we will see tomorrow.

THINK AND PRAY: Make a list of the good things that God has given you. So when you pray today you can thank God for your family and for warm, safe homes and many other things.

DAY 8

Jochebed's Baby is Found

Read: Exodus 2:5-9

D o you remember where Jochebed had left her baby? Yes, in a basket in the reeds beside the river. Do you remember who was watching over him? Of course, it was his sister Miriam.

The daughter of Pharaoh came to the river (we would call her a princess). She saw the basket and asked her maid to bring it to her. The baby was crying and the Princess felt sorry for him. Miriam came out from where she was hiding. She asked the Princess whether she would like someone to take care of the baby. When the Princess said that she would, Miriam called her mother.

What a surprise for Jochebed. Instead of being afraid of someone taking the baby away, she was now being asked to look after him. The Princess actually said she would give her money for doing this.

Jochebed took her baby home and cared for him. She did not need to hide him, because now the Princess would protect him. Jochebed was able to keep her little boy until he was old enough to leave her. She knew that she must then take him to the Princess. The Princess took him as her own son and she named him Moses.

In the New Testament we read that Amram and Jochebed were not afraid of what Pharaoh had said about the little boys (Hebrews chapter 11 verse 23). They trusted God and did what was right. God had a very important job for Moses to do when he had grown up.

THINK AND PRAY: God had plans for Moses' life. He has plans for your life too. When you pray today, thank God that He knows all about every family, just as He knew about the family we have been reading about today.

DAY 9

Rahab and the Spies

Read: Joshua 2:10-11

Yesterday we learned about Jochebed's baby, Moses. When he grew up, Moses was chosen by God to bring the Israelites out of Egypt. We can read all about this in the Book of Exodus.

The Israelites knew that God was going to give them the land of Canaan to live in. God had promised this to Abraham many years before.

The people who lived in Canaan at that time worshipped idols and did many wicked things. God had given them hundreds of years to change their ways, but they did not change.

There was a city in Canaan called Jericho. Jericho had high, strong walls all around it. The walls were so thick that houses could be built on them. The people thought that their strong walls would keep them safe.

Rahab lived in Jericho and her house was on the city wall. The people who lived in Jericho had heard a lot about the Israelites. You read this in today's Bible verses. Rahab believed that the God of the Israelites was the true God. She believed that God would give the land of Canaan to them.

One day two men came to Rahab's house. They had been sent by Joshua, who was now the leader of the Israelites. They were spies, sent to find out what Jericho was like.

The King of Jericho heard that two men had been sent by the Israelites to spy out the land. He sent men to Rahab's house to find them. Rahab hid the two spies and kept them safe.

THINK AND PRAY: Rahab lived in Canaan where people bowed down to statues. Rahab believed in the true God. She showed that she believed by helping the Israelites. Ask God to help you believe in him and to help other believers too.

DAY 10

Rahab's Request

Read: Joshua 2:12-13

Rahab knew that the Israelite soldiers would come and fight against Jericho. She thought about her family: her father and mother and her brothers and sisters. Was there a way that their lives could be saved?

Rahab spoke to the two spies about this. She had helped them. Would they help her? Would they make sure that she and her family were kept safe? Rahab wanted the men to promise this.

The spies explained to Rahab that there were two things she must do and one thing she must not do, if she wanted to be safe. Rahab had a scarlet (red) cord. She was going to use it to let the men escape out of the window. This cord must be fastened in the window when the Israelites came. The second thing Rahab must do was to bring her family into her house. If any of the family went outside into the street, the men could not promise that they would be safe.

Then there was the one thing Rahab must not do. She must not talk to anyone about the two spies. She must not tell anyone that they had been in her house. She must not tell anyone what they had said. She certainly should not tell anyone which way they went when they left Jericho.

Rahab helped the spies to get away without anyone seeing them. She let them down by the cord out of her window. She also told the men where they should hide until it was safe for them to go back to their own people.

Tomorrow we will learn whether Rahab did as the spies told her she should.

THINK AND PRAY: We have a great and wonderful God. When you pray today, thank God that you can learn about Him from the Bible. Remember Rahab, who believed in the true God, even though she had not been taught about Him.

DAY 11

Rahab is Saved

Read: Joshua 6: 20 and 23

The people of Jericho were afraid. They had heard how God had helped the Israelites when they left the land of Egypt. Now the Israelites were camped in their tents near to Jericho.

One day there was the sound of trumpets and marching feet. The Israelite army was marching all the way round the city. Then, all was quiet again. The next day the same thing happened: trumpets sounding and feet marching, then quiet again. For six days the Israelites marched once each day around Jericho.

The seventh day came. The sounds went on much longer. The Israelites marched seven times around the city. The walls were strong, the city gates were locked. Would the soldiers think that the walls of Jericho were too strong for them? Would they stop marching and go away?

Suddenly the Israelites gave a very loud shout. The walls that the people thought would save them, fell down. God was helping the Israelites to take the city for themselves.

Do you remember where Rahab's house was? It was on the city wall. But Rahab was safe. She had done as the two spies had told her. Her family were with her in the house. The scarlet cord was tied in her window.

The two men came to Rahab's house. They led her and her family away from Jericho. They brought them near to their own camp.

In the New Testament we read that it was by faith that Rahab's life was saved (Hebrews chapter 11 verse 31). Rahab trusted God when the people living around her did not believe in the true God at all.

THINK AND PRAY: God helped the Israelites in a very difficult situation. He can help you too even when things seem impossible. When you pray today, ask God to help you to trust Him so that you will not be afraid, whatever happens.

DAY 12

Deborah the Judge

Read: Judges 4:4-5

A long time ago a woman called Deborah lived in the land of Israel. It was not a happy time. There were enemies in the land who made life hard for the Israelites. The enemies were King Jabin and his soldiers, who were led by a man called Sisera.

The Israelites remembered that they had not been obeying God. They prayed that God would help them. God was kind to His people. When they were truly sorry that they had disobeyed Him, He sent someone to help them.

The Bible tells us that Deborah was a prophetess and a judge. That means that God spoke to Deborah so that she could tell the people what they should do. Being a judge meant that people could come to her when someone had done something wrong. Deborah would know who was telling the truth. She would say what must happen to the person who had done wrong.

God told Deborah that it was time for the Israelites to fight against their enemies. She sent for a man named Barak. Deborah explained to Barak that he must lead the Israelite soldiers. They must fight against King Jabin.

Barak said that he would do as God said if Deborah would go with him. If Deborah would not go, then Barak said he would not go either.

Deborah told Barak that she would go with him to the battle. Barak knew that it would help him to have Deborah there. She would tell him what God wanted him to do.

THINK AND PRAY: Deborah was brave to promise to go with Barak to the battle. She was brave because she knew that God would be with her. Ask God to give you courage to face what happens in your life.

Day 13

Deborah Goes to the Battle

Read: Judges 4:14

Deborah kept her promise and went with Barak to the place where the battle would be. Do you remember who led King Jabin's soldiers? It was Sisera. These soldiers were ready to fight against the Israelites. They had a very strong army, with lots of horses and chariots.

Deborah told Barak when it was the right time for the battle. She reminded him that God would be with him to help him. Israel won the battle. Even Sisera got out of his chariot and ran away. He came to the tent of Jael and Heber. Only Jael was there and she invited Sisera to come in and rest. She pretended to be kind to him. While he was asleep, she killed him. King Jabin and his army would not be able to harm the Israelites any more.

Chapter 5 of the book of Judges is like a long poem. It is the song that Deborah and Barak sang because they were so thankful to God. They were thankful that their enemies, who had seemed so strong, had been beaten. They knew that this was because God had helped them.

All through the book of Judges we read about times when the Israelites stopped obeying God. Each time this happened, their enemies became stronger than them. When they were in trouble they prayed to God. God chose leaders called Judges, to help the Israelites. All those leaders, except Deborah, were men. As we have already learned, Deborah was chosen to be a prophetess as well as a judge.

THINK AND PRAY: God will not ask you to be a prophetess like Deborah. God has given us the Bible where we can read all that God wants us to know. The Bible is God's Word. It is true and you can trust it. Pray that as you read the Bible, God will help you to understand and remember what you have read.

DAY 14

Ruth Moves to Bethlehem

Read: Ruth 1:16-17

Ruth lived in the land of Moab. She did not learn about God, because the people of Moab were idol-worshippers.

A family from the land of Israel came to live in Moab. They were Elimelech and Naomi and their two sons Mahlon and Chilion. Their home was in Bethlehem, but there was a famine there. They travelled to Moab because they thought they would not have enough food if they stayed where they were.

Mahlon and Chilion both got married in Moab. Mahlon married Ruth and Chilion married Orpah. Life became very sad for this family. Elimelech died and then Mahlon and Chilion died. A woman whose husband dies is called a widow. The family was now three widows with no one to care for them.

One day, Naomi heard that there was plenty of food in Israel: the famine was over. She decided she would go back to her home. She set out with Ruth and Orpah with her.

However, Naomi did not like to think of Ruth and Orpah going to a land that would seem strange to them. She told them that it would be better for them to go back to their home in Moab. Ruth and Orpah cried. They did not want Naomi to be lonely. At last Orpah went back down the road to Moab.

But, Ruth would not leave Naomi. The verses you read today were her promise that she would never leave her. She had learned to trust in God. She knew now that idols were no use at all. They could not hear prayers or help the people who prayed to them.

Ruth and Naomi came to Bethlehem. The people who knew Naomi were excited to see her again.

THINK AND PRAY: People in some countries still pray to idols. They need to know about the one true God and his Son, Jesus Christ. Ask God to send more men and women who will go throughout the world to tell others about the Lord Jesus.

39

DAY 15

Ruth is Treated Kindly

Read: Ruth 2:11-12

Naomi must have been glad to be back in Bethlehem. She was not lonely because Ruth was with her. But it was very different from when she had lived there with her husband and her two sons.

Ruth and Naomi were poor. How could they buy food and other things they needed?

God had taught the Israelites to be kind to poor people. At harvest time, the farmers were to leave some grain, corn, wheat or barley in the fields for the poor. People who needed food could take what grew in the corners of the field. They could also take anything that was dropped by the reapers. This was called gleaning.

Ruth told Naomi that she would go to the fields to glean, because it was the time of the barley harvest. Ruth came to the field of a man named Boaz. She followed the reapers who were gathering the barley.

When Boaz came to see how his workmen were getting on, he saw Ruth. He spoke kindly to her: you can read some of his words in today's Bible verses.

Gleaning was hard work, bending down to pick up the grain under the hot sun. Boaz was kind to Ruth and made sure she had enough to eat and drink. He also made sure she had gathered plenty of grain.

When Naomi saw how much Ruth had brought home, she knew someone must have been kind to her. When Ruth told her that she had been in Boaz's field, Naomi was pleased. She explained to Ruth that Boaz belonged to Elimelech's family. Naomi said thank you to God that Ruth had found her way to the field that belonged to Boaz.

THINK AND PRAY: Ruth came to Boaz's field out of all the fields around Bethlehem. That's amazing. She trusted God and He was guiding her. Ask God to guide you throughout your life in things you have to decide and friendships you make.

Day 16

Happier days for Ruth

Read: Ruth 4:14-16

Yesterday we learned that God cared for the poor people. He made sure that they could have enough food. God had given another law to His people: a law about widows;

At the time when Ruth and Naomi lived, life was very hard for a lady whose husband had died. God's laws said that a widow could be married to someone belonging to her husband's family.

This would usually be the nearest relation to the man who had been her husband. There was one man in Naomi's family who was a nearer relation than Boaz. When Boaz asked him if he wanted to marry Ruth, he said no. This meant that Boaz could ask Ruth to marry him. He was a rich man and able to buy back all the land that used to belong to Elimelech and his sons, Mahlon and Chilion. So Ruth and Boaz were married.

Ruth and Boaz had a baby boy. What a happy time it was for Naomi. She had been very sad when she first came back to Bethlehem. Now she had a little grandson to care for. The little boy was named Obed.

If you look at the first page of the New Testament, Matthew chapter 1, you will see Boaz, Ruth and Obed's names in verse 5. When Obed grew up he became the grandfather of King David, who was a great King in the land of Israel. Many years later the Lord Jesus was born into this family (Matthew chapter 1 verse 16).

When Ruth travelled to Bethlehem with Naomi, she could not have known that one day her name would be in that wonderful list.

THINK AND PRAY: The story of Ruth is wonderful. God looked after Ruth in amazing ways. He taught her about Himself. Thank Him that people who are taught to pray to idols can learn to trust in the true God, like Ruth did.

DAY 17

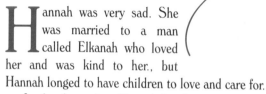

Hannah's Prayer

Read: 1 Samuel 1:11

Hannah was very sad. She was married to a man called Elkanah who loved her and was kind to her., but Hannah longed to have children to love and care for.

In the days when Hannah lived, a man could have more than one wife. This was not how God wanted families to be. When it happened, it always made someone unhappy. Elkanah married two wives: Hannah and Peninnah. Peninnah did have children to care for. She was very unkind to Hannah and made her feel even more sad.

Every year, Elkanah took his family to the Tabernacle at Shiloh. This was the place where the Israelites went to worship God before the temple was built.

The tabernacle was a very special tent with golden furniture inside it. Long ago, when Moses led the

Israelites, God had told him how the tabernacle should be made. When the Israelites were travelling, they carried the tabernacle with them. When they settled down in the land of Canaan, it stayed in Shiloh.

One day, when they were at Shiloh, Hannah was crying and could not eat her meal. Elkanah did not like to see Hannah so unhappy. When the meal was over, Hannah went to the tabernacle. Eli the priest was sitting by the doorway. Still crying, Hannah began to pray. She told God about her sadness and then she made a promise. If God would give her a little boy, she would give him to God.

Hannah did not pray out loud, but her lips moved. Eli thought that Hannah had had too much wine. He spoke to her about drinking too much. Hannah explained that she had not taken any wine. She had been telling God all about her troubles.

THINK AND PRAY: Remember that when you pray you can tell God about anything that troubles you, like Hannah did. Share your troubles and concerns with God today because he cares for you.

47

DAY 18

Hannah Keeps Her Promise

Read: 1 Samuel 1:27

Eli the priest had made a mistake about Hannah. He saw that she had really been praying. He spoke kindly to her and said he hoped God would give her what she had asked for.

When Hannah went back to her family, she did not look sad any more. Nothing had changed, but Hannah was trusting God to answer her prayer.

The next day, the family went back to their house in Ramah. Some months went by and then Hannah had a baby boy. She called him Samuel, a name that means 'heard of God'. Hannah believed that God had heard her prayer and given her the son she had been wanting so much.

Do you remember what Hannah had said in her prayer? She had promised that if God gave her a little boy she would give him to God. Hannah had not forgotten her promise. While Samuel was a baby, she stayed at home when Elkanah went to Shiloh. But as soon as Samuel was old enough to eat ordinary food, Hannah took him to Shiloh.

While the family were there, Hannah spoke to Eli the priest. She told him that here was the child she had prayed for. Samuel was to stay at the tabernacle and learn to help Eli.

THINK AND PRAY: Do you think that when Hannah went home she forgot about Samuel? Of course not. We know that she loved him and thought about him. She made new clothes for him and took them with her each year when she went to the tabernacle. When Samuel grew up, God chose him to be the next leader (Judge) of the Israelites. He would help the people right up to the time they had their first king. God had answered Hannah's prayer in a very wonderful way. When you pray, trust God to hear your prayer, as He heard Hannah's.

DAY 19

Abigail - A Wise Woman

Read: 1 Samuel 25:18 and 32

Abigail was married to a very rich man called Nabal. Nabal was rich but he was not a good man. He was not kind to other people.

Abigail and Nabal lived in the land of Israel at a time when the Israelites had settled down there. They had a King called Saul. Saul had disobeyed God. God chose a young man named David to be the next King after Saul.

King Saul was so jealous of David that David had to move to places where the King could not find him. He gathered a group of strong men to be with him.

Nabal owned lots of sheep and goats. David and the men who were with him helped Nabal's shepherds. They made sure that none of the animals were stolen or lost.

When David heard that Nabal was having a feast day he sent ten of his men to see what Nabal would give them, for all the help they had given his shepherds. Nabal spoke roughly to David's men and would not give them anything.

One of Nabal's workmen told Abigail what had happened. He warned her that David and his men were angry with Nabal.

Abigail collected together a very large present of food for David and his men. This was what you read about in the first of today's Bible verses. She took some of her servants with her and went to meet David.

David said thank you to God that Abigail had come to meet him. She stopped him harming Nabal because he was angry with him. He and his men were grateful for the present she had brought.

THINK AND PRAY: The Bible says that Abigail was a woman of good understanding. That means she understood what was the right thing to do. Pray that God will give you the sort of understanding that Abigail had.

DAY 20

The Widow of Zarephath

Read: 1 Kings 17:9-10

Ahab the king of Israel, did many wrong things. He married a very wicked woman named Jezebel. She worshipped an idol called Baal and Ahab built a temple for Baal.

God sent Elijah the prophet to Ahab. He told Ahab that there would not be any rain to make the crops grow. This was because the people had disobeyed God.

After this, Elijah lived beside a brook for a while, but the brook dried up because there was no rain. God told Elijah to go to Zarephath where a widow would give him food. You will remember that a widow is a lady whose husband has died.

As you read in today's Bible verses, Elijah met a widow when he arrived in Zarephath. He asked her for a drink of water. Then he called to her to bring him some bread as well.

The poor widow told Elijah that all she had was a little flour and oil. She was out collecting sticks to make a fire. She planned to bake her last loaf on the fire. This would be all that was left for her and her son to eat. The widow thought that after that, they would die.

Elijah told the woman to bake her bread and bring some to him. Then he had something very surprising to tell her. Elijah told her that God would not let her flour and oil run out until He sent rain.

Would this poor widow believe what Elijah had told her, or would she keep her last little bit of food for herself? She did believe. We know this because she did exactly what Elijah had told her to do.

THINK AND PRAY: The poor widow had hardly any food in her house. Do you remember to thank God every day for enough to eat? Say a short prayer before you eat your meals thanking God for your food.

DAY 21

What the Widow Learned

Read: James 5:17-18

The verses you read today tell us that at this time it did not rain in Israel for three years and six months. That is a long time and the ground would have been very dry. Nothing could grow properly, so there was a famine in the land: not enough food for the people.

God had promised that the widow's flour and oil would not be used up until He sent rain. God always keeps His promises. Every day the widow found enough flour and enough oil. She had given Elijah a room in her house so that he could stay there. There was enough food for the widow and her son and for Elijah.

One day, the widow's son became very ill. We don't know how old he was, but his illness got worse and he died. The widow spoke to Elijah. She thought that she was being punished for something that she had done wrong. Elijah carried the boy to his room. He prayed that God would let him live. God heard Elijah's prayer and gave life to the boy. Elijah took the boy to his mother. How amazed she must have been to see her son alive and well again.

Think of the things that had happened to this lady since Elijah came. Her little bit of flour was not used up and there was always enough oil. Then something even more wonderful: her son was alive again.

The widow learned two things. She realised that Elijah was 'a man of God'. She came to understand that Elijah spoke the words that God gave him. (I Kings chapter 17 verse 24)

THINK AND PRAY: When you read the Bible, you are actually reading God's words to you. That is wonderful! Pray that God will help you to understand that the Bible is different from other books. It is the best book!

DAY 22

A Widow in Trouble

Read: 2 Kings 4:2

Elisha was a man who God chose to be a prophet after Elijah. A group of men came to Elisha because they knew he was a prophet. They wanted to be with him and to learn from him. One of these men died and the lady who had been his wife was in great trouble.

This widow found that there was a debt that she could not pay. Do you know what debt is? It is when you borrow money from someone. Your debt is the amount of money that you need to pay back.. We do not know why this family had to borrow money. Probably it was because they did not have enough money to buy the things they needed. When her husband died, the person they had borrowed from, wanted the widow to pay the money back.

The man the widow owed money to did not take pity on her because she was poor. He said that if she did not pay, he would take her two sons to be his slaves. This would be very bad for the widow and for her sons. She would be very lonely without them. She would also be very sad, thinking of them being slaves. Being a slave meant belonging to someone and always having to do what they said.

The widow knew what she must do. She must go to Elisha: he would help her. Elisha asked her what she had in the house. As you read in today's Bible verse, all she had was a jar of oil. Elisha told the widow that she must borrow a lot of empty jars—anything that would hold oil. Then she must shut the door and pour her oil into all the jars she had borrowed.

THINK AND PRAY: The widow we have read about today knew who to go to with her troubles. We can tell God about anything that troubles us. Tell God about anything that concerns you today. Ask him to forgive you for your sins.

DAY 23

The Widow's Oil

Read: 2 Kings 4:7

Yesterday we learned about a widow who was in great trouble. She knew that she should go to Elisha the prophet for help. She showed that she trusted God to help her by doing exactly what Elisha told her to do.

First of all the widow borrowed as many empty jars as she could. Then she and her sons went into the house and shut the door. The two sons began to hand the jars, one by one, to their mother. The widow took her own jar of oil and poured some into the first jar. Then she poured oil into the second jar and then the third. The oil just kept coming until every jar was full. How had this happened? We would call it a miracle: something that only God could do. Long ago God made the world and everything in it. He was able to make more oil for this poor widow who trusted Him.

The widow told Elisha what had happened. He told her to sell the oil, so that she would have money to pay back what she owed. This was wonderful. Her sons would not have to leave her. They would not lose their freedom by having to be someone's slaves. The widow would have no more debt. Elisha said that the money she had left would be for her and her sons. They would be able to buy food and other things that they needed.

THINK AND PRAY: God does not always work miracles to give people what they need. He helps boys and girls and grown-ups to know what they can do for people who need help. Thank God that He knows everyone who trusts in Him, whether they are rich or poor.

DAY 24

The Woman from Shunem

Read: 2 Kings 4:10

There was a lady who lived with her husband in a town called Shunem. We do not know her name, but she is usually called the Shunammite woman. Sometimes Elisha passed her house and she would invite him to come in for a meal. She called Elisha 'a man of God'. She knew that God had given him a special job to do. Of course, you will remember that we have already learned that Elisha was a prophet.

One day the lady asked her husband if they could make a room for Elisha to stay in. Travelling in those days was not easy. Elisha would be glad to have somewhere to rest when he passed that way. An upstairs room was made ready for him. In the room, the Shunammite woman put a bed, a table, a chair and a lamp.

Elisha thought about the kindness he had been shown. He asked his servant, Gehazi, to call the woman. When she came, he tried to find out if there was anything he could do for her. The Shunammite woman was quite content. She did not ask for anything.

Afterwards, Gehazi told Elisha that the woman had no sons. Her husband was quite old: older than a man would usually be when a baby son was born.

Elisha told the Shunammite woman that she would have a little boy. About a year later her baby boy was born. She must have been very happy to have a little one to care for.

THINK AND PRAY: It's good to be kind to others. You don't have to wait until you have grown up to do this. Even boys and girls can be kind and helpful. When you pray, ask God to help you to be kind to other people as the Shunammite woman was.

DAY 25

Elisha's Prayer is Answered

Read: 2 Kings 4:18-19

The baby boy we read about yesterday grew bigger just as you have done. One day, when he was old enough, he went to his father in the field. It was harvest time and the reapers were busy gathering in the crops. The little boy began to call out: his head was hurting. His father asked a servant to carry him home to his mother. Of course there was no ambulance and no hospital to take him to.

The Shunammite woman sat with her little boy on her lap. He had become very ill and she could not help him. The little boy she loved so much, died. She carried him to Elisha's room and laid him on the bed. She then went to tell her husband that she needed to see Elisha. She knew that it was Elisha, the man of God who could help her.

The woman took a servant with her and went as quickly as she could to the place where Elisha was. At first Elisha wondered what she wanted. When He understood what had happened, he sent Gehazi on ahead. Gehazi could not help the boy.

Elisha went with the Shunammite woman. When they reached her home, he went to his room and prayed. He held the little child against him until the child became warm. God answered Elisha's prayer and the boy became alive again. Gehazi called the Shunammite woman. When she came, how she must have thanked God when she saw that her little boy was alive.

THINK AND PRAY: God does not always work miracles when people are ill. Thank God that He has given us bodies that can heal (get better). Thank Him too for doctors and nurses who help us when we are ill.

DAY 26

The Little Captive Girl

Read: 2 Kings 5:2-3

It is hard to imagine what it would be like to be taken away from your home to another country. This did happen to a little girl who lived in the land of Israel many years ago. Soldiers from the land of Syria came into Israel and took her to Syria.

The little captive girl was taken to the home of a very important man. His name was Naaman and he was in charge of the King of Syria's soldiers. The little girl became a servant to Naaman's wife. She learned that Naaman had a bad illness called leprosy.

We might think that this little girl would not really care about Naaman being ill. After all, his soldiers had taken her away from her home and her family. She must have missed her family and her home very much. But she did want to help Naaman. She told Naaman's wife about

Elisha the prophet. She was sure that if Naaman could go to see Elisha, he could be healed.

Naaman told the King of Syria what the little girl had said. The King wrote a letter for Naaman to take to the King of Israel.

When the King of Israel read the letter that Naaman brought he was very upset. The letter said that he should heal Naaman from his leprosy. The King knew that he could not do that. He thought this would make the King of Syria very angry.

Elisha heard about what had happened. He told the King to send Naaman to him.

THINK AND PRAY: The little girl was in a strange land. Instead of thinking of her own troubles, she thought of how she could help Naaman. She believed that God could make him well, through Elisha the prophet. Ask God to help you love and care for others and to love Him most of all.

DAY 27

How Naaman was Made Well

Read: 2 Kings 5:14-15

Naaman travelled to the house where Elisha lived. He thought Elisha would come out to meet him where he was waiting by the door. He thought that Elisha would call on God and that a miracle would happen: his leprosy would be healed.

Nothing happened as Naaman expected. Elisha did not come to see him. He sent a message: go and wash seven times in the River Jordan, then you will be healed.

Naaman was angry. He said that there were better rivers to wash in in the land of Syria. Naaman would have gone away still angry, but his servants spoke to him. They said that if he had been told to do some great thing, he would have done it. So why not do this simple thing. In this way they persuaded him to do as Elisha said. So Naaman went down to the River Jordan and dipped himself in the water seven times. When he came out of the water, the leprosy had gone.

How different Naaman felt when he went back to Elisha's house. It was wonderful to know that he was well again. But something else had happened to him. He now believed that Elisha's God was the only true God.

Naaman wanted to give Elisha a present, but Elisha would not take anything. He knew that it was not him but God who had healed Naaman.

We do not know what Naaman's wife said when Naaman got home. She must have been so happy to see him well again. All this had happened because of the words of the little captive girl.

THINK AND PRAY: Do you know what it means to be unselfish? It means to think of other people more than yourself. Remember the little girl we have been learning about. Pray that God will help you to be unselfish as she was.

DAY 28

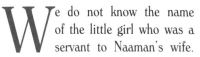

Learning from Naaman and the Little Captive Girl

Read: 1 John 1:9

We do not know the name of the little girl who was a servant to Naaman's wife. We do not even know how old she was. Her true story is in the Bible because she told Naaman's wife about Elisha. We have thought about how unselfish this girl was when she could have spent her time feeling sorry for herself. She was also brave. The people of Syria worshipped idols. This little girl was not afraid to speak about God's prophet who lived in the land of Israel.

Naaman could not make himself better. When he did what Elisha told him to do, God healed him. Did you know that we all have something that is worse than leprosy? Boys and girls and grown-ups have sinful hearts. This is why we do wrong things like telling a lie or hurting someone.

The Lord Jesus took the punishment for the sin of everyone who trusts in Him. He will forgive us and He will teach us to do right things. We do not have to go on a journey like Naaman did. We can pray just where we are. We can ask God to forgive our sins and make our hearts clean.

THINK AND PRAY: Maybe you are reading this and you are already a Christian. You know that God has forgiven your sin and you want to do what pleases Him. Think about the little captive girl who told Naaman where to go for help. Do you have friends who need to hear about the Lord Jesus? If you are not sure what to say to them, could you invite them to Sunday School, or a children's meeting? Pray that God will help you to think about others as the little girl we have been learning about did.

DAY 29

The Aunty who Saved a Life

Read: 2 Chronicles 23:11

Jehosheba was the sister of King Ahaziah. Ahaziah was king of the part of the land of Israel called Judah. Jehosheba was married to Jehoiada who was the High Priest at the temple.

Ahaziah was not a good king. He had learned evil things from his mother, Athaliah. He was only king for one year and then he died.

When a king dies, one of his children, usually the oldest boy, becomes the next king. Athaliah had a terrible idea. If she killed the king's children, she could be the queen and rule the land. It is hard to even think of someone killing their own grandchildren. But this is what she did.

Long before, God had made a promise to King David. God had said that there would always be a king from his family. Was it possible that God could not keep this

promise because of an evil woman? God always keeps His promises: He always does what He says He will do.

Jehosheba saw what was happening. She could not save all her brother's children. However, she did save one little boy whose name was Joash. Joash was just one year old.

Jehoiada and Jehosheba hid little Joash in a room in the temple. They kept him hidden for six years. They had to hide him to keep him safe from Queen Athaliah.

When Joash was seven years old he was crowned king. Of course he did not know how to do everything that a king must do. As long as Uncle Jehoiada was alive, he helped Joash.

God knew all about that wicked woman Athaliah. He helped Jehosheba to save little Joash, so that Judah would have its king.

THINK AND PRAY: Remember when you read a promise in the Bible - God always keeps his promises. When you pray today, thank God that there is nothing that can stop Him keeping His promises.

DAY 30

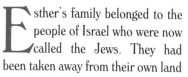

Esther Becomes Queen

Read: Esther 2:17

Esther's family belonged to the people of Israel who were now called the Jews. They had been taken away from their own land by the Babylonians. Esther lived in the land of Persia. Her mother and father had died: she was looked after by her cousin, Mordecai. He must have been quite a lot older then Esther. He brought her up as if she was his own daughter. The Bible tells us that Esther was very beautiful.

One day, Esther was told that she must go to the palace of King Ahasuerus. A lot of young women had been sent for. The king wanted to choose a new queen. He had been very angry with Vashti who used to be the queen.

Out of all the beautiful young women in Persia, King Ahasuerus chose Esther to be his queen. Esther did not tell anyone that she belonged to the Jewish people. Mordecai had told her not to.

There was a very important man in Persia whose name was Haman. He liked everyone to bow down to him. Mordecai would not bow down and Haman became very angry with him. Haman knew that Mordecai was a Jew. He decided not to punish Mordecai. Instead, he would try to destroy all the Jews in the lands that belonged to King Ahasuerus.

Haman told lies about the Jews to the king. The king believed what Haman said. A day was decided on which all the Jews were to be killed.

When Mordecai heard the news, he was very sad. Queen Esther's maids told her how sad Mordecai was. Esther sent someone to find out what was wrong. Mordecai sent a message to her so that she would know about the plan to kill the Jews.

THINK AND PRAY: There are still evil people like Haman. Find out about places in the world where Christians are not allowed to read the Bible or go to church. Pray that God will protect Christians in countries where people would hurt them.

DAY 31

Queen Esther's Feast

Read: Esther 5:2

Mordecai told Esther that she must go to King Ahasuerus. She must plead with him to stop the destruction of the Jewish people.

Esther explained to Mordecai that no-one was allowed to go to the king, unless they were sent for. Anyone trying to get into the king's room could be put to death. Only if the king held out his golden sceptre would the person know they were safe. (A sceptre is a stick of gold which is held only by the king to show his power.)

Mordecai told Esther that she might have been made queen in order to help the Jews at this time. Esther knew that she must go to the king, as Mordecai had asked. She told him to gather the Jews together to fast (go without food) for three days and to pray for her. Mordecai did as Esther had requested.

Esther stood in her beautiful royal robes, where the king would be able to see her. The king was sitting on his throne. He held out the golden sceptre to Esther. Esther went nearer to the throne and touched the sceptre.

King Ahasuerus asked Esther what it was that she wanted. She asked the king if he and Haman would come to a banquet (feast) that she had prepared for them. They came and Esther gave them wine to drink. But Esther did not tell the king that day what it was that she wanted. She asked that they would come again to her feast the next day.

THINK AND PRAY: King Ahasuerus was so powerful that he might kill anyone who he did not want to see. But God is greater than any king. Thank God that although He is so powerful, we need never be afraid to pray to Him.

DAY 32

The Jewish People are Saved

Read: Esther 7:3

It was the second day of Esther's feast. The king and Haman had come as she asked. Now was the time when she knew she must speak to the king about her people, the Jews. Esther pleaded for her life and the lives of all the Jewish people. The king wanted to know who it was who would dare to harm them.

This was a dangerous moment for Esther. Haman had been the king's favourite. The king had made him the second most important person in the land. What should she say? Bravely, Esther told the king that the enemy of the Jews was Haman.

King Ahasuerus was very angry. At last he realised that he should not have trusted Haman. Haman was very, very frightened. He had set up a great tall wooden frame to hang Mordecai on, so that he would die. The king gave orders that Haman should be hanged instead.

The laws of Persia could not be changed. So the king asked Mordecai and Esther to write a new law. This law said that on the day the Jews were to be destroyed, they could fight back against their enemies. The Jews would be safe: they could protect their homes and their families.

There was another change in the land of Persia. Mordecai was given the important job that had been Haman's. No one in that land would ever dare to try to harm the Jewish people again.

THINK AND PRAY: Remember that God still hears and answers our prayers today, as He did in Esther's day. He is the same yesterday, today and forever. Pray for Jewish people who live in the land of Israel now. Ask God to help them to understand that the Lord Jesus is the promised Saviour. Ask God to help them to trust in Him.

DAY 33

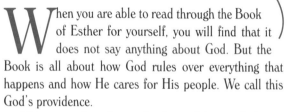

**Learning from the Book
of Esther**

Read: Romans 8:28

When you are able to read through the Book
of Esther for yourself, you will find that it
does not say anything about God. But the
Book is all about how God rules over everything that
happens and how He cares for His people. We call this
God's providence.

There must have been other beautiful young ladies in
Persia, beside Esther. Mordecai understood that Esther
had been made queen for a special reason (Esther chapter
4 verse 14). King Ahasuerus chose Esther. In a way that
we cannot understand, God was making sure that Esther
was in the right place to help the Jewish people.

There was a time when some men were plotting
against the king. Mordecai found out and saved the king's
life, but King Ahasuerus did not know this. The night
before Esther was going to ask the king to save the Jews,

the king could not sleep. He sent for someone to read to him. The man read from a book about all that happened in Persia. He read about Mordecai saving the king's life.

By the time the king went to Esther's second feast day, he knew that what Haman had said about the Jews was not true. Mordecai had saved his life. The king not being able to sleep seems a very little thing. But it was God's providence that the king should begin to find out the truth.

God had promised long ago to send the Saviour into the world through the family of Abraham. The nation of Israel came from Abraham's family. God would not allow the people of Israel to be destroyed.

THINK AND PRAY: As we are learning, nothing can stop God doing what He says He will do. He is all powerful and always keeps his promises. When you pray today, thank God for all we learn from the Bible that helps us to trust Him more.

DAY 34

Good news for Elizabeth

Read: Luke 1:13

Elizabeth was married to Zacharias the priest. They had no children, but they had prayed that they would one day have children to care for. As they grew older, it did not seem that they would ever have a family.

One day, when Zacharias came home from the temple, he could not speak. Elizabeth must have wondered what had happened to him.

Something very special had happened in the temple that day. The angel Gabriel had appeared to Zacharias. He told him that Elizabeth would have a baby boy who they must call John. The angel explained that when John grew up, he would have a special job to do. He would make people ready for the coming of the Saviour, the Lord Jesus.

Zacharias asked the angel how he could know that this was true. He was thinking about how old he and

Elizabeth were. He found it hard to believe that Elizabeth would have a baby after so many years had gone by. Zacharias was told that he would be unable to speak until the baby was born. This was because he had not believed the angel's words.

Soon Elizabeth knew that she was going to have a baby, just as the angel had said.

About three months before the baby was due to be born, Elizabeth had a visitor. A relative of hers, maybe a cousin, came to stay with her for a while. This was a young lady called Mary, who was also waiting for a Baby to be born. (We will learn about Mary later.)

THINK AND PRAY: Elizabeth loved God and trusted God even though she waited a long time for her prayers to be answered. Ask God to give you patience as you wait for His answers.

DAY 35

Elizabeth's Task

Read: Luke 1:63-64

At last the day came when Elizabeth's baby was born. Now she had a little boy to love and care for. When he was eight days old, it was time to give him a name. Elizabeth's friends and relations thought he would be called Zacharias after his father. Elizabeth said that he should be called John. Everyone looked at Zacharias to see which name he wanted the baby to have. Zacharias still could not speak, but he wrote the words 'his name is John'. After he had done this, he was able to speak again.

Zacharias began to thank and praise God for all that He had done for His people. His words showed that he understood what John's task would be. People who lived near to Zacharias and Elizabeth thought about all that had happened to them. They thought about how Zacharias suddenly became able to speak again. They knew that there must be something very special about the little boy who had been born.

Elizabeth knew all about God's promise to send someone special into the world. He would be the Saviour of everyone who trusts in Him. She understood that when John grew up, he would tell people to be ready for the Saviour. How careful she must have been looking after the little boy. She knew that God had given her the task of caring for him while he was young. She and Zacharias would have taught John many things from the Old Testament books.

THINK AND PRAY: The Bible says that we should tell God all about the things we need. Ask God to make you like Elizabeth so that you will trust God even if He does not answer your prayers quickly. God knows far better than we do, what is best for us.

DAY 36

Mary's Visitor

Read: Luke 1:38

Mary lived in the City of Nazareth, in the land of Israel. She was engaged to be married to a man named Joseph.

One day Mary was visited by the angel Gabriel. This was just six months after Elizabeth knew that she was going to have a baby, as the angel said. Whenever we read in the Bible about angels coming from heaven, we know that they brought very important messages.

The angel told Mary that she would have a baby boy whose name would be Jesus. He would not be an ordinary baby with an ordinary father. This Baby would be the Son of God.

The angel then told Mary about Elizabeth. Mary told the angel that she was God's servant: she would do whatever God asked of her. Soon after the angel's visit, Mary went to stay with Elizabeth, because Elizabeth was a relation of hers.

Zacharias and Elizabeth, and Mary and Joseph, were people who loved God. They believed all the promises which God had made in Old Testament days. They knew that God would send someone into the world to save us from our sin and evil.

When Mary arrived at Elizabeth's house, God helped Elizabeth to know something about Mary's Baby. Elizabeth knew that this Baby was the Person who God had promised to send. Mary praised and thanked God for all that He had done.

THINK AND PRAY: How good it must have been for Mary to be able to stay with Elizabeth for a while. Mary was probably quite young and she would have found Elizabeth to be a great help to her. When you pray today, thank God that He did not send the angel to a rich or important person. God chose a young lady who loved and trusted Him. He gave her the very special task of caring for God's own Son when He was born.

DAY 37

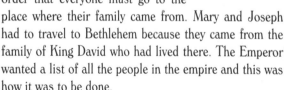

Mary's Journey

Read: Luke 2:7

Mary had to go on a long journey before her Baby was born. The Emperor (who was called Caesar Augustus), gave an order that everyone must go to the place where their family came from. Mary and Joseph had to travel to Bethlehem because they came from the family of King David who had lived there. The Emperor wanted a list of all the people in the empire and this was how it was to be done.

Mary's Baby was born while she and Joseph were in Bethlehem. They were far from their own home, with no crib or soft blankets for the Child. The inn was full and so there was nowhere comfortable to stay. Baby Jesus was laid in a manger that usually would have held food for the animals.

In the night some shepherds came to see Mary, Joseph and the Baby. What could have made them leave their sheep that night? An angel had appeared to them and told them the good news. The Saviour had been born in Bethlehem. The shepherds hurried to find the Child the angel had told them about. When they had seen the Baby Jesus, they told lots of people about Him. The people were amazed at what the shepherds told them.

Long ago, about seven hundred years before the Lord Jesus was born, the prophet Micah had written about Him. God helped Micah to know that the Saviour would be born in Bethlehem. We can read this in Micah chapter 5 verse 2.

Mary lived in Nazareth, but she had to travel to Bethlehem. The Emperor did not know that his order meant that the Saviour would be born exactly where Micah had said.

THINK AND PRAY: God is in control of everything. We can see him at work throughout the whole Bible and history. Thank God for the wonderful way He keeps His promises.

DAY 38

**Anna Sees the
Promised Saviour**

Read: Luke 2:37

nna was an old lady. When she was young she had been married, but her husband had died just seven years after their wedding. So Anna became a widow. It must have been a sad time for her, but Anna loved and trusted God.

We do not know how Anna spent the years after her husband died. The Bible tells us about her when she was eighty-four years old. She loved to be in the temple. She loved to pray, and she knew all about the promises God had made.

Anna knew the Old Testament: the first part of the Bible we have today. (The New Testament was written after the Lord Jesus went back to heaven.) Right through the Old Testament there are promises from God. These promises are all about the Saviour who God would send.

One day, Anna saw a man and woman with their Baby, in the temple. Baby boys were brought to the temple when

they were about six weeks old. This was something God taught His people to do. Anna did not know Mary and Joseph, but she looked at the Baby they had brought. God helped Anna to know that this Baby, Jesus, was the promised Saviour. Anna said a prayer of thanks to God.

Anna had been waiting to know that God had done what He had promised. She knew that there were other people in Jerusalem who were longing for the Saviour to come. Anna knew who these people were because they loved and trusted God as she did. She went to tell them about the Child she had seen in the temple.

THINK AND PRAY: The Lord Jesus has promised that He will come to earth again (John chapter 14 verse 3). Ask God to help you to love and trust the Lord Jesus as Anna did. Then you will look forward to seeing Him one day.

DAY 39

Visitors from a Far Country

Read: Matthew 2:1 and 11

After the Lord Jesus was born, Mary and Joseph stayed in Bethlehem for a while. They had found a house where they could stay. One day, some men who had travelled a long way, came to the house. The Bible calls them wise men from the East. We do not know how many there were. Back in their own land, these men had seen a star. Somehow they knew that this star was special and it meant that a special King had been born in the land of Israel. They set out to find Him. They went to the palace of King Herod at Jerusalem.

The king was not at all pleased to hear that a new king had been born. He knew very well that the Jewish people were waiting for God to send the Saviour. He sent for the priests and the scribes–men who knew the Old Testament well. He asked them where the Saviour would be born. They told him what Micah the prophet had said in Micah chapter 5 verse 2: Bethlehem.

King Herod told the wise men to go to Bethlehem and search for the Child. Then they would be able to tell him where he could go to worship the new King. The wise men saw the star that they had seen in their own land. It led them to the house where Mary was with the Lord Jesus.

The wise men brought out precious gifts of gold, frankincense and myrrh (expensive beautiful perfumes made from plants).

THINK AND PRAY: What a surprise for Mary when she saw the travellers. How amazed she must have been when they bowed down to worship the little Boy. Ask God that you may love the Lord Jesus as Mary did. Pray that you may welcome Him into your life as the shepherds and the wise men welcomed Him when He came into the world.

DAY 40

Another Journey for Mary

Read: Matthew 2:13

Mary and Joseph did not know that they were in any danger. But God knew the heart of King Herod. In a dream God told the wise men not to go back to King Herod. They obeyed God and went back to their own land a different way.

An angel spoke to Joseph in a dream. He told Joseph to take Mary and the Child Jesus into the land of Egypt. King Herod was going to try to find Jesus and destroy Him.

Mary was already away from her own home in the city of Nazareth. Now, Joseph told her they must leave the land of Israel and travel to Egypt where they would be safe from King Herod. They must set out in the night. How quickly Mary must have had to gather their belongings together. How hard it was to set out on a long journey to a land they did not know.

The special task that God had given Mary was not an easy one. We know that she trusted God because she and Joseph did whatever God told them they must do.

Without a car, bus, train or aeroplane they travelled more than two hundred miles. God protected them. They arrived safely in Egypt where they would have had to find somewhere to stay. Mary probably did not have to stay very long in Egypt. King Herod died and once again an angel spoke to Joseph in a dream. This time it was to tell him that it was safe to return to the land of Israel.

Mary and Joseph with the Lord Jesus, set out on the long journey back. They went to the City of Nazareth and so were back among people they knew.

THINK AND PRAY: Think about all the places in the world that you could go. God is there too. He is everywhere. Ask God to help you so that you may obey what He says in the Bible, as Mary and Joseph obeyed God's messages brought by the angel.

DAY 41

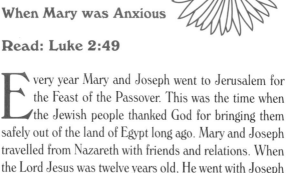

When Mary was Anxious

Read: Luke 2:49

Every year Mary and Joseph went to Jerusalem for the Feast of the Passover. This was the time when the Jewish people thanked God for bringing them safely out of the land of Egypt long ago. Mary and Joseph travelled from Nazareth with friends and relations. When the Lord Jesus was twelve years old, He went with Joseph and Mary to Jerusalem. It was a long journey of about eighty miles and the roads would have been hot and dusty. Some people may have had a donkey to ride on or to carry their food and other belongings.

After staying some days in Jerusalem, the people from Nazareth set off for home. They travelled for a day. Jesus was not with Mary and Joseph but they were not worried about Him. They felt sure He was with friends and relations.

At the end of the first day's travel Mary and Joseph looked for Jesus among their friends but they did not find

Him. Where could He be? Now they were really anxious. They went all the way back to Jerusalem. They searched for three days.

At last, Mary and Joseph came to the temple. There they saw a group of men who were teachers. These were men who knew a lot about the Old Testament. In the middle of the group they saw Jesus. He was listening and asking questions. Everyone who heard Him was amazed at how much He understood.

Mary told Jesus how anxious she and Joseph had been. You read Jesus' answer in today's Bible verse. The Lord Jesus knew that God was His Father: He must do what God wanted Him to do.

THINK AND PRAY: Mary did not quite understand what Jesus said. It can be difficult sometimes for us to understand the Bible but God gives wisdom and understanding. Pray that God will help you to keep on trusting Him, even when things happen that are hard to understand.

DAY 42

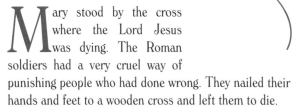

Mary's Saddest Day

Read: John 19:26-27

Mary stood by the cross where the Lord Jesus was dying. The Roman soldiers had a very cruel way of punishing people who had done wrong. They nailed their hands and feet to a wooden cross and left them to die.

The Lord Jesus had never done anything wrong. He never spoke a wrong word or even had a wrong thought. The leaders of the Jewish people hated Jesus. The people listened to Jesus and saw the wonderful things He did. The leaders were jealous. They decided He must die.

The Lord Jesus was the Son of God. He could have asked God His Father to send angels to rescue Him. He did not do this. He came into the world to take the punishment for the sin of everyone who trusts in Him. As He hung on the cross in great pain, Jesus saw His mother. He understood how sad she was, as she saw Him suffer so much. One of the disciples, Jesus' special friends, was also standing nearby. His name was John.

Jesus told Mary that John would be her son. He told John that Mary would be his mother. Jesus knew that John would be the person who could comfort Mary better than anyone else. John took Mary to his house.

This was a time of great sadness for Mary. She remembered all the wonderful things that happened when Jesus was born. She knew that He had made many ill people better. He had made blind people see and lame people walk. Now He was dying.

Bravely, Mary stood by the cross when many of Jesus' friends had gone because they were afraid.

THINK AND PRAY: Our sin stops us knowing God as our Friend. Thank God that the Lord Jesus died so that our sins can be forgiven, and we can know God as our Friend.

DAY 43

Great Joy for Mary

Read: Acts 1:13-14

On the third day after Jesus died on the cross, there was wonderful news. He was alive: He had risen from the dead. This is the most wonderful news in the world. It means that for everyone who trusts in the Lord Jesus, death will not be the end of life. They will live with Him for ever.

What did Mary say when she heard what had happened? The Bible does not tell us. We can only imagine what joy she felt. How she must have given thanks to God.

Some people tell us that Mary was perfect: that she never sinned (did anything wrong). This is not true. Everyone born into the world, except the Lord Jesus, has sinned. Mary called God her 'Saviour' (Luke chapter 1 verses 46-47). Only sinners need a Saviour, because they need to have their sins forgiven. Mary trusted and obeyed

God. She carried out the task God had given her. It was a great honour to be chosen by God to care for Jesus in His early years.

Forty days after Jesus rose from the dead, He went up into heaven. We call this 'the ascension'. After this, Jesus' special friends, the eleven disciples, met in an upstairs room. They met to pray together. As you read in today's Bible verses, Mary was with them. This is the last time we read about Mary in the New Testament.

Mary had loved and cared for the Lord Jesus when He was a Child. Now she understood so much more, she loved and trusted Him as her Saviour.

THINK AND PRAY: How wonderful it is that the Lord Jesus is alive for ever in heaven. Say thank you to Him because you know He hears you when you pray.

DAY 44

A Woman Made Well

Read: Mark 5:33-34

There was a woman who had been ill for a very long time. The doctors she had seen could not help her. She had spent all her money on trying to get well. But she was no better, in fact her illness got worse.

This poor woman heard about the Lord Jesus, who made ill people well. She was afraid to speak to Him, but she had a plan. If she could get near enough to touch the hem, the bottom edge, of His robe, she believed this would heal her. She believed that Jesus was so powerful that even touching His clothes, could make her well.

There was a crowd of people around the Lord Jesus when this ill woman came to the place where He was. She was determined to make her way through the crowd. At last she stood behind Jesus. She put out her hand and touched the hem of His robe. She was sure no one had seen her. She felt the illness leave her: she knew that she was well again.

Jesus asked who had touched Him. His friends, the disciples, were surprised He asked, as so many people were pressing around Him. The Lord Jesus knew that someone who needed help had touched Him.

The lady trembled at having to speak with such a crowd of people around. She bowed down to Jesus and told Him all that had happened. The Lord Jesus spoke kindly to her. He said that she was made well because of her faith. She had believed that the Lord Jesus was able to make her well and He had done so.

THINK AND PRAY: Think about how powerful God is. What has God done to show us his power? Ask God to help you to trust the Lord Jesus, like the woman we read about today.

DAY 45

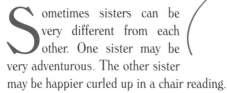

Mary and Martha

Read: Luke 10:41-42

Sometimes sisters can be very different from each other. One sister may be very adventurous. The other sister may be happier curled up in a chair reading.

Mary and Martha were sisters who lived in the village of Bethany. (This is not the same Mary as the one we have already learnt about.) They had a brother called Lazarus. When the Lord Jesus lived on earth, He had no home of His own. Mary and Martha welcomed Him to their home. It was good that Jesus could spend some time there away from the crowds. We learn how different the sisters were from reading what happened one day when Jesus came to their house.

Martha was busy preparing a meal. Maybe she wanted it to be a specially good meal that day. She saw that Mary was sitting quietly listening to the Lord Jesus. She began to feel upset that she had so much to do and Mary was not helping.

Martha asked Jesus to send Mary to help her. Jesus spoke kindly to Martha, but He did not tell Mary to help. He said that Mary had made the right choice to listen to His words.

Do you feel a little bit sorry for Martha? She was working hard without any of the things we have in our homes. No electric or gas cooker, no microwave, no fridge, not even a tap to get water easily and quickly.

The Lord Jesus gently showed Martha that the time He spent with them was important. There was such a lot that only He could teach them. A simple meal was all that was needed.

THINK AND PRAY: Mary and Martha were very different but they both loved and trusted the Lord Jesus. He understood them and loved them both. Thank God for his love for you, a sinner. Thank God for how he has made you different from everyone else you know.

DAY 46

Sadness and Joy

Read: John 11: 21 and 32

Mary and Martha's brother Lazarus was ill. They knew just what to do. They sent a message to the Lord Jesus. Jesus did not hurry to Bethany. He waited two days before He set out. But before he left he already knew that Lazarus had died.

Martha heard that Jesus was coming and went to meet Him. Mary stayed in the house. Martha told Jesus that if only He had been there, her brother would not have died. She believed that Jesus could have made him well.

As Jesus talked to Martha, she told Him that she knew that He was the Son of God. Martha understood this when many people did not understand.

Martha told Mary that Jesus was asking for her. Mary hurried out to see Him. She said the same words as her sister had done: if only Jesus had been there, Lazarus would not have died.

The Lord Jesus asked where the body of Lazarus had been placed. They showed Him the grave. This was a cave with a stone across the opening. Jesus asked for the stone to be taken away. While Mary and Martha and their friends watched, Jesus prayed and then called Lazarus to come out. Lazarus did come. The Lord Jesus had given him life.

Mary and Martha may have been disappointed that Jesus did not come quickly when Lazarus was ill. But the Lord Jesus knew what He would do. Mary and Martha saw something more wonderful than their brother being made better. They saw that the Lord Jesus was able to give him life. What a wonderful day in their house.

THINK AND PRAY: God does not always answer our prayers straight away. Pray that you may be patient and trust that God knows best.

DAY 47

Mary Shows her Love

Read: John 12:3

Martha was busy again. This time an evening meal was being prepared. Mary, Martha and Lazarus were all there and the Lord Jesus and His disciples had come to have supper.

It was good that Jesus was always made welcome by this family. Many people did not welcome Him, especially the leaders of the people. They were jealous when they saw the crowds listening to Jesus. The Lord Jesus knew all about this. He also knew that it would soon be time for Him to die on the cross.

We have already learned that Mary and Martha were different in their ways. Martha showed her love for the Lord Jesus by making Him welcome and serving a good meal. How could Mary show her love for Him?

Mary had something precious. It was some beautifully scented oil, from the spikenard plant. It cost a lot of money. It was usually only used on special occasions. She took all the oil and poured it over Jesus' feet. The house was filled with the lovely perfume.

One of the disciples, Judas, grumbled about what Mary had done. He said the oil could have been sold so that the money could have helped poor people. Judas did not really care about the poor: he used to steal money.

The Lord Jesus understood that Mary was showing her love to Him. He said that people could help the poor anytime, but He would not always be with them.

THINK AND PRAY: We cannot do what Mary did: the Lord Jesus is in heaven now. If we know Him as our Friend and Saviour, we will want to show our love to Him by what we do. Pray that God will help you to give glory to Him by being generous and kind to others.

DAY 48

Lydia Listens

Read: Acts 16:14

It is not very often that people say that purple is their favourite colour. However, there was a time when people wanted to buy material that had been dyed purple. In a city called Thyatira in the country we call Turkey, the people had found a way to make a purple dye and their purple cloth was very popular.

Lydia came from Thyatira and she sold purple cloth. When we read about Lydia in the book of Acts, she was living in the city of Philippi, in the country we know as Greece. Beside the river outside the city, she met with some other women, to pray. One day some men came to talk to these women. They had travelled there to tell people about the Lord Jesus. One of the men was Paul and he had with him his friends, Timothy, Silas and Luke.

Lydia believed in the true God but she did not know about the Lord Jesus. She listened as Paul spoke about

Him. We do not have Paul's words but we know what he taught wherever he went. He would have spoken about Jesus dying on the cross to save everyone who trusts in Him. He would also have told the women how Jesus rose from the dead and went back to heaven.

As Lydia listened, God helped her to understand and believe Paul's words. She trusted the Lord Jesus to be her Saviour.

Lydia invited Paul and his friends to come and stay at her house. She was glad to be able to help them, as they had travelled so far.

They knew that she was now a Christian and they must have been very glad to have her help.

THINK AND PRAY: If you go to church, find out whether the church helps any missionaries. If so, find out where these missionaries are. Pray for missionaries who travel all over the world to tell people about the Lord Jesus.

DAY 49

Priscilla the Tentmaker

Read: Romans 16:3-4

Priscilla lived with her husband Aquila in the city of Corinth. They were Jewish people who had become Christians. They used to live in Rome, but the Emperor had said that all the Jews must leave Rome. So they had to move.

Priscilla and Aquila were tentmakers. That was how they earned money to buy the things they needed.

One day Paul arrived in Corinth. We learned a little about him yesterday. He was a missionary, travelling to different places to tell people about the Lord Jesus. But Paul also knew how to make tents, so he stayed with Priscilla and Aquila. He joined them in their work.

Paul stayed a year and a half in Corinth and then he set out by boat for Syria. Priscilla and Aquila came with him part of the way.

Priscilla and Aquila stayed in the city of Ephesus while Paul continued on his journey. In Ephesus they heard a man called Apollos teaching people about God. He knew the Old Testament books very well, but he did not know very much about the Lord Jesus.

Priscilla and Aquila talked with Apollos. They explained to him all that Jesus had done. Now that they had helped him, Apollos would be able to teach others.

In New Testament days, Christians did not have special buildings to meet in. They met in each other's houses. While Priscila and Aquila lived in Corinth, Christians met in their house.

The Bible verses you read today, show how much help Priscilla and Aquila gave Paul. Not only Paul, but many Christians were grateful to them. Priscilla and her husband were ready to help others whenever they could.

THINK AND PRAY: We need to learn about God and trust in Jesus Christ so that we can bring the truth of God to others. Ask God to help you to be like Priscilla–always ready to help others.

DAY 50

Lois and Eunice

Read: 2 Timothy 3:15

We have read a little about Paul, who travelled many miles to tell people about the Lord Jesus. You may remember that when he came to Philippi, he had with him a young man named Timothy. The Bible helps us to understand how Timothy became someone Paul could trust to help him. Paul also trusted him to teach others about the Lord Jesus.

Timothy's mother's name was Eunice and his grandmother was Lois. Both Eunice and Lois had become Christians. They knew that it was important to teach Timothy from the Bible while he was very young. We can think of Timothy, even when he was a little boy, listening to his mother or his grandmother.

Timothy would have learned from them about all that had happened in Old Testament days. He would have heard about the first man and woman, Adam and Eve. He would have learned about how they disobeyed God and so sin came into the world. Lois and Eunice would have taught Timothy God's great promise, to send a Saviour.

Lois and Eunice did not have the New Testament to read, but they had heard about the Lord Jesus. They believed that He was the One God had promised to send. They had trusted Him to be their Saviour. This meant that they could explain to Timothy that God had kept His promise. He had sent His own Son, the Lord Jesus. He was the promised Saviour.

Paul knew that Timothy had been taught very well from the Old Testament. He had been taught so well, that he understood why he should trust in the Lord Jesus. Paul saw that Timothy was a young man who he could take with him on his travels.

Eunice and Lois prepared Timothy for the work God gave him to do.

THINK AND PRAY: Lois and Eunice taught Timothy about God. Who teaches you about God? Can you teach others? When you pray today, thank God that you are learning from the Bible, like Timothy did long ago.

By the same Author

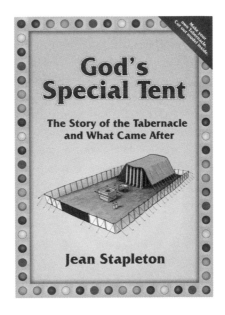

ISBN: 978-1-84550-811-1

Do you like tents? Perhaps you've gone camping, staying in one place and then moving to another. God's people the Israelites lived in tents in the wilderness as they moved from Egypt to the Promised Land. God gave them instructions about how to make a special tent – where He could be present among His people. Find out about how they made this tent and what special furniture and curtains were placed inside it. How did they build the tent and how did they carry it from one place to another? The priests made sacrifices to atone for the sin of the people, but the tabernacle or tent of meeting was a place that taught the people about the one who was going to save them from their sin for good – Jesus Christ, the promised Messiah. His sacrifice would mean that no other sacrifices were needed and that people could worship God all around the world.